# Learn To Swim

By

Benjamin Roberts

**First Published 2012.**

**Published by Wiggly Worm Publications**

**Revised edition 2015**



Book design and edit by www.Pumpkin-Spice.co.uk. Drawn artwork and Illustrations by Ann-Marie Fripp.

ISBN 978-0-9573908-1-2

Also availiable as an ebook - ISBN 978-0-9573908-0-5

Visit **www.theswimmingteacher.com** for more information.

# Contents


| | | |
|---|---|---|
| Acknowledgements | | Page iv |
| Foreword | | Page v |
| Chapter One | Gaining water confidence | Page 1 |
| Chapter Two | Learning to glide | Page 12 |
| Chapter Three | Turning the glide into a swim | Page 19 |
| Chapter Four | Learning to breathe | Page 27 |
| Chapter Five | Putting the swimming and the breathing together | Page 36 |
| Appendix | Printable awards | Page 43 |

# Acknowledgements

There are quite a few people to whom I need to say thank you for the part they played in helping me to write this book. Firstly I must start at the beginning with my wonderful Parents Lynfer and Donald because they were the ones who taught me to swim and at such an early age that I can never remember a time when I could not swim. They encouraged my love of the water and ensured that I was given ample opportunity to swim, to scuba dive, to sail, to snorkel, to row and just generally enjoy all that the water has to offer.

I would like to thank my beautiful and amazing Wife Danielle for supporting me in everything that I do and for always being there for me. I would also like to thank my baby son Oscar for melting my heart a hundred times a day and for making me smile more than I ever thought possible. I also have two adorable young step children, Corey and Kelsey and consider myself fortunate enough to have been the one who taught them how to swim and am so proud of them. In fact the illustrated character that appears throughout the book is actually modeled on Corey, something he is very pleased about! I am the proudest Husband, Father and Step Father there is!

I am also so grateful for all of the help, understanding and patience shown by the staff of Pumpkin Spice who managed the technical side of the book including the creation of the website and the Android App which accompanies it and the wonderful illustrations that appear throughout.

Finally I must thank every single person that I have ever taught to swim. For me, it has and always will be a pleasure but without your efforts, your courage, your commitment and your patience, the whole process would not have worked. Learning to swim is not always simple and straight forward. Whether they are children or adults if someone has a genuine fear of the water, meeting this fear head on and pushing through it takes a real bravery and no teacher can teach someone to be brave. It's simply something a person finds deep within themselves. I have so much respect for each and every one of you.

# Foreword

I would argue that learning to swim is as important as learning to read or write. This might sound dramatic but when you consider the amount of drowning victims each year, hopefully my argument becomes a lot more understandable. Although water does, and always will, present a potential hazard the danger can be minimised. Learning to Swim is one of the most important ways of doing this along with educating our Children about the risks. The earlier in life that a person learns to swim, the more of their life they can spend enjoying the water safely.

I have spent the past twenty years of my life working as a Swimming Instructor and in this time I have taught thousands of children and adults to swim and I have no intentions of stopping! However, during my time I have realised that not everyone can afford to pay for swimming lessons and that some people either enjoy the challenge of teaching themselves to swim or the rewards that come from teaching their own children to swim.

This book has been written mostly for the latter of these two groups and whichever one you fall into, I can ensure you that Parents, Step Parents, Grand Parents and so on who wish to teach their children to swim can do so successfully by following information within this book. My approach, which I will happily share with you, does not rely on the use of buoyancy aides and it definitely does not expect Dad to place one hand on his child's belly while they splash furiously with their hands and feet!

The methods I use, which are tried and tested, revolve around the idea of teaching the learner about their own buoyancy, rather than strapping artificial devices to them. We focus on what I call breath control, and ensure that the learner fully understands how to take a huge controlled breath and why they need to do so. Taking a huge inward breath is not as simple as it sounds, especially to a nervous child. However, it will increase the body's ability to float and will decrease the panic that the learner experiences when they submerge their face into the water during the early stages. We then combine this new breathing skill with two shallow water practises. The first involves learning how to perform a 'star float' and the second being able to crawl in the water using the hands only. Once these are achieved the actual teaching of the swimming stroke is easy!

If I had to pick my area of expertise, it would be taking nervous non-swimmers and building their confidence by giving them practises in which they feel in control of the situation. Shallow water is all that is needed to learn to swim. If you think of it, a swimmer only uses the top few inches of the water so why then should we take our learner out of their depth and take away their feeling of control?

The idea behind the book is simple. I teach you how to teach your child to swim. The text is easy to follow and the illustrations are aimed at the child, so they can look and see what is expected of them. All you need to do is to read each relevant section before your practise session begins and have plenty of patience! I promise it does work and my methods will make the process far easier than you would imagine.

# Chapter One

## Gaining water confidence

Regardless of age, learning to swim without being confident in the water is a near impossible task. Even if the pupil does learn to swim, they will never truly enjoy swimming and therefore will miss out on countless opportunities throughout their lives. I would say that this Chapter is perhaps the most important in the whole series as it lays the foundations for the rest of the programme. How long it will take to gain water confidence depends on how nervous your child is, however two things are certain. Firstly this stage cannot be rushed and secondly you will realise when the pupil becomes water confident by the way they approach the practices that are set. Now let's get started!

### Step 1:- Getting used to goggles and learning to take a HUGE breath!

First things first, I am one of those swimming instructors who believes in the use of goggles when teaching someone to swim, especially a beginner. If someone is nervous in the water then, in my experience, encouraging them to submerge their face with their eyes closed will increase the fear. They will only see darkness and as the saying goes, 'the worst fear is the fear of the unknown'. Equally encouraging our pupil to open their eyes in the pool without goggles will result in chlorine irritation which is not pleasant and can result in a soreness and itching of the eyes. For these reasons I would strongly advise that you buy a nice comfortable pair of goggles, ideally with a soft silicone style seal around the eyes and an adjustable nose piece. The older foam sealed goggles do not offer as good a protection from the water and tend to perish far sooner.

When you have found the right goggles, and believe me there are lots of 'child friendly' versions out there, you must first adjust the goggles to fit so that they are not too tight, but equally tight enough to serve the purpose. There should be no visible gaps between the eye sockets and the seal. Check the seal around the nose area closely as this is a common area for leakage as a tiny gap may be present here. I prefer goggles that have an adjustable nose strap as opposed to the fixed nose type to avoid this problem. Also make sure that the rubber strap that goes around the head sits just above the ears and during any of the practises, never falls below it. If the strap does slide down the eye pieces will not get the correct pull into the eye sockets.

When you have got the goggles fitting just right you might find your child does not like wearing them and it is not uncommon for children to pull them off at every opportunity! An ideal introduction to wearing goggles is to encourage the pupil to wear them in the shower or the bath, especially when washing the hair. The main benefit of this for our learner is that the shampoo will not be able to enter the eyes. However, what is more important to us is the fact that it will introduce to our pupil the concept that goggles actually protect the eyes from the water and allow the wearer to see under water. It is good that this initial practice is also carried out in an environment in which the pupil feels at ease, namely their own bathroom!

Just before we try the practise in the shower let us fully understand what we mean by the phrase 'take a big breath' and understand why this is so crucial to the success of the whole program. I've taught well over two thousand people to swim and most of these were children under the age of seven. Most of these young children could simply not understand the concept of getting a big breath. Some of them would breath out as much as they could, thinking that this was what I wanted. Some of them had a big breath in but then blew it out straight away and others thought that a 'small hiccup' style breath was enough. Many simply tried too hard to get a huge breath and this resulted in a loud squeaking or creeking sound. Neither is correct as both drastically reduce the amount of air that the body can take in. Try it for yourself!

Therefore we should assume that our pupil knows nothing! Show them what you mean and get them to look at your mouth and how wide open it becomes. Tell them to listen to the sound it makes when you take this inward breath. The noise by the way should be a long yet calm inward breath, as if you were about to do a big sneeze but don't blow out! Use your hands to show how your chest gets bigger as the big breath goes into your chest. Then hold your breath for just a few moments. Now tell our pupil to copy you and ask them if they could feel their chest get bigger. Make sure they are aware that they do not need to hold their breath for long and as soon as they want to breath normally again, they can.

This is one of the most important things a non-swimmer can learn. Why? Put simply buoyancy is everything and the more oxygen we can get into the body the better it will float. When we get to this stage you will see for yourself! Also when a beginner puts their face into the water, if the oxygen levels within their body are high, then they will not experience panic anywhere near as quickly as they would if they had not had the big breath.

Let's progress the practise now by moving it into the shower. Begin by telling our learner to take a big breath and to close their mouth tightly. They must then tilt their face upwards towards the shower head so that the water splashes over the face. Once the pupil can look up into the shower in a controlled manner with no signs of panic, we can advance the practice by encouraging a gentle submersion under the bath water. Please remember, always carry out these practises with supervision.

**Congratulations your child has just earned Award Certificate 1 (See Appendix)**

Always emphasise the big breath before putting the face into the water and ensure that the mouth stays closed. This sounds like common sense but when people are nervous or scared their breathing pattern alters and it is not uncommon for a nervous beginner to submerge their face and gasp under water due to panic. This in turn causes them to swallow water and cough. The pupil only needs to stay submerged for a few seconds at a time. Any longer would lead to unnecessary panic and risk. Therefore make the practice open ended. For example, instead of telling the pupil to try and stay under water for 10 seconds, tell them to stay under the water for as long as they are comfortable.

You can still make a game of this by counting the length of the submersion and try to beat their previous time. This way, they know that they are in control of the situation and you will see the confidence and the times increase as a result.

For younger children this is a good moment to introduce water toys. This could be their favourite character figure such as Barbie or an Action Man or indeed a specially designed water toy. The purpose of the toy is simply to distract the pupil from their fear of the water and to allow them to concentrate on something else which in turn makes the submersion longer without them realising it!

Key phrases: - Goggles on, big breath, mouth closed tight and eyes open.

## Step 2:- How to perform controlled submersions at the pool.

When arriving at the poolside, always seek advice as to the depths of the different areas of the pool. The lifeguards should be more than willing to advise you. All we need is shallow water, no deeper than chest depth on your child. Without increasing the depth walk around the pool, holding hands, until our learner feels confident enough to walk unassisted, though always accompanied by you. Remember some pool bottoms are very slippery so take extra care.

Once this has been done, try to find some 'Roman style' steps, which are ideal for sitting on. If your local pool does not have these then the poolside offers a suitably secure holding point. We need to ensure that our nervous learner feels safe and holding or sitting onto something secure makes the whole process feel far less daunting. Remember, try to understand what our scared young child is feeling and bare in mind that they must feel in control of the situation.

Revisit the submersion practices which were learned in the bath with the goggles on! The process is exactly the same. Continue to emphasise the key phrases, 'big breath' and 'lips closed tight'. The face goes gently into the water to avoid it going up the nose or into the goggles. Again only a few seconds of 'face in' practise at a time and our learner must always know they can lift their face as soon as they wish.

The more this is done the more relaxed the pupil will become and the more control they will show. As the confidence grows, water toys can be introduced to make the whole process more enjoyable. Make sure the child has their goggles on correctly and that they also have their eyes open under water! As I said, remember sinking toys are a wonderful way of distracting children who are nervous as they tend to forget their fears and focus on the toy. Another advantage of sinking toys is that the pupil must open their eyes to reach under the surface and retrieve the objects.

**Congratulations your child has just earned Award Certificate 2 (See Appendix)**

Key phrases: - Big breath, eyes open and lips closed tight.

## Step 3:- Forever Blowing Bubbles!!

Once the controlled submersion has been mastered, we will advance it one more stage. Continue to reinforce the use of one of our key phrases, that of the 'big breath'. However, on this occasion we will not hold the breath and keep the lips closed tightly. Instead, as soon as the face touches the water, we will encourage the pupil to blow outwards, thus creating bubbles.

We will give this the key phrase of 'big bubbles'. Again the face should only be submerged for a few seconds at a time. When blowing the bubbles, the best example of a good technique is to compare the blowing of bubbles to the blowing out of candles on a birthday cake, i.e. A big breath in followed by a long controlled breath out into the water. When blowing bubbles correctly water cannot come into the mouth. Once this is mastered, keep it at the back of your minds as we do not need it until a later stage but keep practising it!

Key phrases: - Big breath, big bubbles and blow out the candles!!

Step 4:- Learning to float.

When our learner can submerge their face into the water in a controlled manner, without swallowing any or panicking, they are ready for step 4 in the water confidence series, that of performing a star float. The human body is capable of floating due to a combination of factors including its body fat and the oxygen that is stored within the body itself.

However there are several different factors that can affect how well a person can float. Firstly comes confidence. If a learner is very nervous they are going to be tense rather than relaxed and being relaxed, is a key part of successfully learning to float. The body is far more buoyant when spread out in a listless crisscross position than it is when it is very tense. The neck and shoulder area should be visibly relaxed. By looking at this area you will be able to tell if the pupil is tense or at ease.

Secondly, our buoyancy increases when our lungs are full of air and oxygen is moving around our body. If you imagine the lungs as footballs, when inflated if footballs were submerged under water they would immediately rise to the surface. Therefore, by using our key phrase of 'big breath' just before the face is lowered into the water, our pupil will not only have a far better chance of performing a successful 'star float' but will also be far less likely to panic than they would if they had not taken a big breath.

When performing a float, we must encourage the pupil to close their lips tightly after the 'big breath' and not to blow bubbles as bubbles would cause the body to gradually sink.

With these pointers in mind, we are ready to try a star float. Again shallow water is needed and roman steps would be ideal. The pupil must put their hands onto either the poolside, the bottom of the pool if the water is very shallow or even a shallow step on the roman style entry steps if you have them. The hands and feet must then be spread as wide apart as possible and when both the hands and the feet are wide apart, from above the body will look like an X. For young children, we always refer to this float as the 'Star Float'.

Our learner then gets the biggest breath they can, seals the mouth tightly and gently lowers their face into the water in a controlled manner. If the pupil pushed their face into the water in an aggressive manner or almost jumped into the position, the bodies momentum would be forced downwards, which in turn would push the body underwater. Obviously it would rise again but this experience can unsettle our learner and we don't want that!

At this point the pupil's legs will usually rise automatically due to the buoyancy. This is probably going to be the first time that our learner has ever experienced 'natural buoyancy' and what is after all, reduced gravity! The feeling will be a strange one as they will have experienced nothing to compare it to. They may therefore take some time to get used to this feeling and make sure you praise them for their efforts!

Don't worry if the floating of the legs does not happen at this stage. As I mentioned earlier, different people have different levels of buoyancy but at this stage if their feet are still on the pool bottom, it's more than likely due to those last few nerves which may cause tension within the shoulders and therefore makes the head a little too high in the water. If the head is lifted even slightly, it causes what I call the 'see saw' effect, namely if one end goes up then the other end goes down. They may also complain of water going up their nose which often goes hand in hand with the lifting of the head and puts a lot of learners off!

To help our learner overcome this problem, simply tell them on their next attempt that when the face is lowered into the water they should try to put their chin close to their chest. This does two things, firstly it will flatten the body out and help the learner float and secondly it will stop the water going up the nose! In fact you can remember that tip for the rest of the process even when they learn to swim. Water only goes up a swimmers nose if they have elevated their head to a position where it should not be!

Once our learners legs are floating on top of the water they must then be encouraged to move their hands from a flat position on the floor (or indeed hands on the step or the poolside) to being on their finger tips. When they are happy in this position they finally have to lift the finger tips off the floor, but very slowly, and then outstretch their arms and hands. At this point the body should float perfectly on the surface. It may take several practise attempts but the feeling of floating should fascinate and intrigue our pupil and ensure that they are happy to continue the practise. Really emphasise the calm nature of lifting the hands. If it happens to quickly they will go downwards rather than staying still on the surface!

Key Phrases: - Big breath, mouth closed tightly and slow, gentle movements.

## STEP 5:- Learning to crawl again!!!

Yes, learning to crawl, this is not a misprint! Once our learner can perform a controlled submersion and a star float, crawling can be a great final step in the confidence series but only if you can find shallow water. When I say shallow water the pupil must be able to place their hands on the bottom of the pool in order to crawl. As a simple guide, the water should not be much deeper than the child's knees. If the water is even a little bit too deep this practice will not work and should not be attempted. A beach style entrance to the water would be perfect, however Roman style steps would also be ideal or even a very shallow pool aimed at toddlers.

Encourage our learner to kneel down and then lean forwards in order to place their hands on the pool bottom. For reference, when the pupil's hands are on the pool floor their elbows should be slightly bent. In this preparation stage, when the child's hands are on the floor, their face should still be above the water line. Therefore the water depth will be enough to ensure that their legs and body can float, but equally it is not deep enough to allow the pupil to feel that they are not in control of the situation i.e. they must be able to regain a standing position if they wanted to.

From an 'all fours' position, encourage the pupil to take their big breath, to gently submerge their face and to crawl forwards on their hands whilst allowing their legs to straighten and then to float up to the surface. The best analogy for a successful movement of the hands and arms is that they should resemble that of an elephant. i.e. big, slow striding movements as opposed to little scurrying movements. As always, when the pupil needs to breathe they should either stop and sit up or if capable, carry on crawling but lift up their head to breathe before placing it back in to the water and continue the practise.

Gradually, as the pupil learns to trust their own buoyancy, this practice will progress into a 'Doggy Paddle 'style stroke. This happens as our pupil relaxes and grows in confidence and this, combined with the crawling action, encourages the pupil to realise that they do not have to touch the floor to crawl through the water.

**Congratulations your child has just earned Award Certificate 3 (See Appendix)**

There is a lot of snobbery towards 'Doggy Paddle' but I would say that this is totally misplaced. In fact, the underwater aspect of 'Doggy Paddle' is very similar to front crawl and if I am totally honest with you my Mother and Father taught me to swim 'Doggy Paddle' before any other stroke when I was about two years of age! If we can get our pupil to swim basic 'Doggy Paddle' at this early stage, then we are well on the way to achieving our aims. Over the next few Chapters you will realise how easily 'Doggy Paddle' can be adjusted and turned into Front Crawl. However, by the end of this Chapter our learner will have learned the fundamental skills needed to swim. Namely the ability to get a huge breath, the understanding of how to float and the technique needed to crawl and swim 'Doggy Paddle'. Well done to you both!

## FREQUENTLY ASKED QUESTIONS

### 1.) Why wear goggles?

In my experience, if a person is nervous of the water, being able to see under the water is a big help. Without goggles, the learner will either keep their eyes closed and never be able to have fun with sinking toys for example, or if they kept their eyes open without goggles they will end up with mild chlorine irritation.

### 2.) Why stay under water for only a few seconds?

Lung capacity increases from birth up to the late teens. Therefore young children cannot hold their breath as long as an adult can. The submersion practises we have looked at are done simply to build confidence. If we encouraged our learner, whether they are an adult or a child, to stay under water for too long, they would experience what we call an 'oxygen debt'. This means that the brain is wondering why the oxygen supply has been cut off. This leads to panic and there is no benefit in putting a pupil in this position. It would, without doubt, hamper the learning process and may well put them off learning to swim.

### 3.) Why shallow water?

Some swimming teachers use what is called the 'Deep water method' to teach a person to swim. In my experience, a learner has to feel that they are still in control of the situation. A learner who is not confident in the water but who can stand up in the water will gain water confidence from our practises far quicker than one who cannot stand up. Safety is paramount and therefore all unnecessary risks should be eliminated and our learner should feel in control always.

### 4.) Why perform the star floats in such a gentle and controlled way?

The human body is buoyant. However if the pupil jumps into the float position, the downward momentum created will encourage the body to travel downwards. Although the buoyancy will counteract this it will take two or three seconds to do so. These vital seconds are wasted and will also eat into the oxygen supplies of the learner and cause panic to set in before the correct position has been achieved. Therefore, it is far easier to do everything correct from the start!!

### 5.) How will crawling assist the learning to swim process?

Crawling in shallow water will help us in several ways. Firstly, even if the head is out of the water and the learner is looking forwards (because they don't yet like their face being in the water) it will give them an understanding of how effortless it is to move through the water. A nervous beginner may be very tense in the arms initially but as they realise the buoyancy is helping to keep them afloat, they will begin to relax. When we can achieve the crawling practise with the face submerged, the learner will soon pick up a natural 'Doggy Paddle' stroke, as they realise that their hands do not need to touch the floor to pull them along. This will in turn give a basic understanding of propulsion and will come in useful in later stages.

# Chapter Two

## Learning to glide.

Once water confidence has been gained and both the Star Float and the Crawling have been mastered, the final step before actually introducing the stroke itself is that of gliding. The purpose of the glide is to give momentum at the start of the swim and to ensure that the swimmer begins the swim in a streamlined position. Gaining this streamlined position from the outset will simply mean that the swimmer feels less resistance in the water and therefore has to put less effort into the actual swim. Swimmers who swim without being in this streamlined position are easy to spot in a public pool as they are the ones who fight their way through the water and thrash and splash with every arm movement! Again, shallow water is all we need for this practise.

### STEP 1:- The position of the legs.

Initially it's easier if our learner gets used to the body position out of the water, whether on the pool side or even at home. Begin with the pupil standing up straight with both feet together and both sets of toes pointing forwards. Ask the pupil to step forward with their favourite foot so one foot is in front of the other but both feet are still facing forwards. Encourage our learner to then bend their knees so that their bottom is almost touching the floor and their front knee is bent nearly at right angles to the floor. The knee of the back foot should be pointing at the floor but not touching actually touching it. Balance must be maintained.

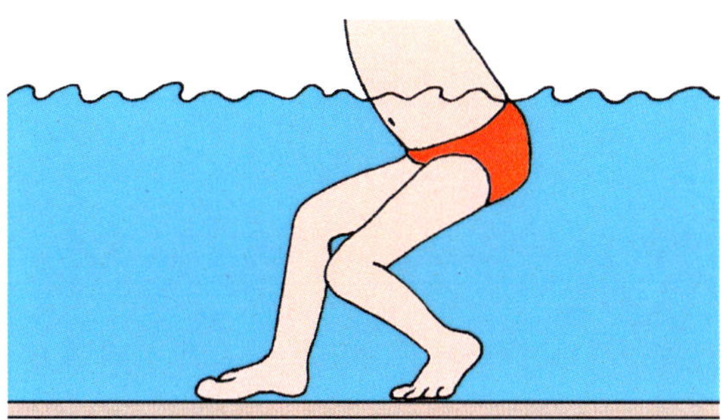

Key Phrases:- Call this position 'Gliding Feet' and emphasise the bend of the knees.

STEP 2:- The position of the arms.

Once the 'Gliding Feet' are in position the arms simply should be outstretched in front of the face with the thumbs together and palms facing downwards. Encourage our learner to keep both arms straight and discourage a bend of the elbows.

Key Phrases:- Straight Arms, palms facing downwards.

## STEP 3:- The Push and Glide.

Our learner should now be capable of performing and holding the gliding start position with knees bent and arms outstretched, outside of the water. If they can then they can attempt the practise in the pool. The water needs to be no deeper than waist deep on the pupil. It is also a good idea to have the pupil facing something solid such as the poolside or roman style steps. My thinking behind this is simply that the learner knows before they begin the glide how far they are expected to glide and hopefully they will feel safer knowing that they are gliding towards something solid.

This fixed target should not be more than one and a half body lengths of the pupil away. A glide that is too long will usually lead to panic and has no real benefit. Remember the whole purpose of the push and glide is simply to give momentum and a streamlined body position at the outset of the swim.

When the pupil enters the pool and gets into the gliding position, their chin should touch the surface of the water whilst their knees are bent and their arms are out stretched. If the water is too deep, this position will be hard to achieve. Also, the deeper the water, the more resistance the pupil will experience when he or she actually begins to push into the glide.

You must then encourage our learner to get the biggest breath they can, to then place their face calmly into the water and finally to gently lean forwards with their hands out in front of them until they reach a position of 'no return' i.e. a forty five degree angle, from which they could not reverse the movement even if they tried.

It is at this point that the pupil should push with both feet and slide across the surface of the water. The leg movement would resemble that of a one hundred metre sprinter bursting out of the blocks. This push of the legs should give sufficient momentum to reach the poolside without a kick of the legs. Encourage the pupil to stretch from their finger tips down to their toes but tell them that they should never ever jump into the glide. If they do, as with the star float, their body will go under water and the practise will be wasted.

Key Phrases:- 'Big Breath' 'Face in the water', 'push', 'slide across the surface' and 'don't jump into the glide'.

## STEP 4:- The Kick.

We are now ready to advance the glide to the next stage and this progression is easy! Sit the pupil on the poolside with their bottom on the edge and their hands leaning on the floor behind them to support their back. Check that our learner's legs are outstretched, their big toes are together, the toes pointed and the feet flexed in a 'tip toe' style position and their knees are kept straight. The legs should be on the surface of the water. The kick is a simple alternating action. As one leg lifts, the other leg lowers. This lifting and lowering action only needs to be two or three inches deep at the very most and neither leg should come out of the water. A common misconception is that the kick should be very fast and as big as possible. Neither is correct. A small kick is ample and a slow relaxed kicking action is all that is needed. If the kick is too big and too fast it will prove counter productive and will waste lots of energy especially when they do learn to swim.

The water around the feet should resemble boiling water in a saucepan i.e. bubbling and not huge uncontrolled splashes. The kick is important in the swim as it gives balance to the stroke and prevents the legs from sinking, but it contributes little if anything to the forward propulsion of the stroke. My favourite way of teaching a good kick when in a sitting position is to compare the movement to that of a drum beat. Explain to the child that their legs are like drum sticks and the water is like the drum. If their legs make big slow movements then the sound of the drum would be the same as a 'Boooom Boooom Boooom', i.e. a big and slow beat. However, if they think of the kick as a drum roll i.e. small yet faster movements then the kick will be just as we want it.

## STEP 5:- The glide and Kick.

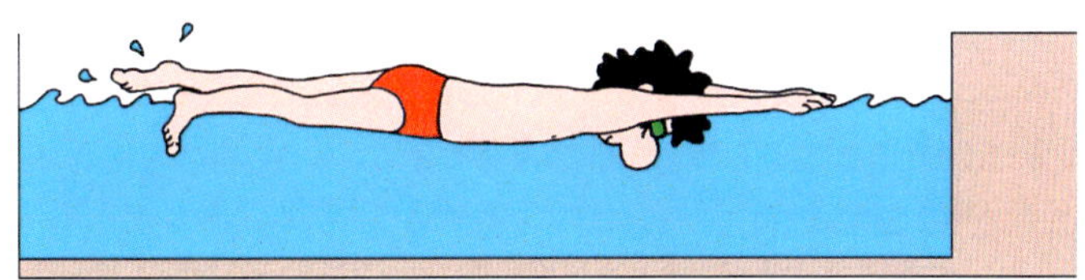

To learn the basic kick should only take a matter of minutes, even for young children. Now, if we get the pupil ready in a gliding position once again tell the pupil that this time they must glide and kick their legs at the same time. Give the instructions 'big breath, face in' followed by 'push'. Again, the distance should not be more than one and a half times the length of the pupils body. As soon as the feet push up from the pool floor, the kick should begin. Once they have learned the kick as a 'drum roll'. I also use the analogy that their legs are now like their engine bubbling away behind them just as an engine does on a speed boat. I always remind them to turn their engine on as they start to push!

Key Phrases:- 'Gliding feet', 'straight arms', 'Big Breath' 'face in', 'push', 'stretch the whole body from finger tips to toes' 'small drum roll kick' and 'straight legs'.

Frequently asked questions:-

1.) What do you mean by 'a position of no return' when starting the glide?

Once our pupil has taken their big breath, put their face into the water and started to lean forwards, they are not ready to push with their legs until they have leaned so far forwards that they could not change their minds and stand up i.e. the point of no return! If the pupil did push before they were in this position they would lift upwards and slightly out of the water.

Therefore, the glide would not be streamlined or smooth and direct forward momentum would be lost.

### 2.) What would happen if my son/daughter did not start the swim with a glide?

A good swim has to start with two things. Firstly the body must be in a streamlined position and secondly there has to be momentum. At this early stage of learning to swim the glide is the only way that our pupil can achieve both. If the swim did start from a stationary position, without any forward momentum, our learner would have to work so hard with their legs and arms that they would tire very quickly, far sooner than a swimmer of equal ability who glides to start their swim. Also if they just went from a standing position to a horizontal position in one movement then the momentum generated would be a downward one rather than a forward one i.e. the swimmer would be sinking.

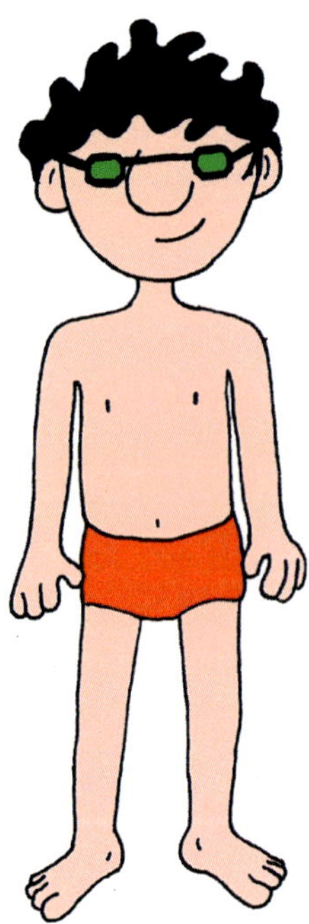

# Chapter Three

## Turning the glide into a swim.

The major difference between a glide and a swim is simple. When performing a glide the arms are outstretched to assist with the streamlined position. Apart from this the arms have no other function. The movement comes from the momentum which is a direct result of the push and glide. However, when a swimmer swims Front Crawl, their arms take on a far more important role and are responsible for the majority of the propulsion.

### STEP 1:- Introducing the Circles.

When teaching a child to swim keeping everything simple is a good idea. For these early stages in the actual stroke itself, we can simply compare the arm action to an alternating circular movement.

The key phrase at this stage is ‘big circles’. As with the earlier lessons initial practises can be carried out at home rather than at the pool. Stand our learner up straight with feet together and toes pointing forwards. The arms and hands should be outstretched in front of the face with the thumbs together and the palms facing down.

**The centre line**

Once this position is achieved, draw an invisible line with your finger from the pupil's nose to the point at which their hands meet. This line should be called the 'Centre Line' and it is vital that this new key phrase is learned and its purpose understood. The 'Centre Line' is so called because it simply splits the body in two halves down the centre.

The reason that we emphasise the use of the 'Centre Line' is simply to ensure that when a swimmer swims front crawl, the circular pull begins and ends on the 'Centre Line' and by so doing, the swimmer will get the maximum power from each and every pull of the hand when performing the stroke.

Not wishing to get to technical but swimming basically follows the teaching of Newton's Third Law of Motion which states that 'each and every action has an equal and opposite reaction'. Put simply, if a swimmer pulls their hand through the water from an outstretched position back towards their body, they would move forwards in an opposite direction to that of the pull. Therefore, the further the pull of the hand, the further forwards the swimmer will be pulled forwards. So don't just teach circles, lets teach our learner to make HUGE circles!

A few common faults with the stroke can be solved by using the 'Centre Line'. One such fault is that swimmers do not pull their hands far enough through the water. Landing on the 'Centre Line' should ensure that the pull is of sufficient length and will give better propulsion. If the hand enters the water several inches off to the side of the 'Centre Line' and begins to pull, then the swimmer will miss out on lots of power when performing the actual swim.

Finally the last common fault which can be solved by using the 'Centre Line' is that of 'Snaking'. 'Snaking' occurs when a swimmer's hand enters the water and begins to pull when it has landed on the wrong side of the 'Centre Line'. Sometimes novice swimmers can be too keen and stretch their hand out past the 'Centre Line'. Therefore each incorrect pull causes a 'snake' like twisting of the body and hampers the streamlined body position.

**The centre line**

Once the pupil is in position and understands where their 'Centre Line' is, encourage them to make the biggest, slowest circles they can but only one arm at a time. It is vital that these circles start and finish on the 'Centre Line'. They must keep their head and body as still as is possible and only move the arms and roll the shoulders. The usual fault at this stage is that some pupils tend to move their head from side to side. This must be discouraged from the outset. If this mistake becomes habit at this stage, it will continue into the stroke when we begin the water practise and will result in the swimmers body twisting itself out of a streamlined position.

In the water, a swimmer's head movement has a direct effect on his or her body. For example, if the head is lifted when performing a star float, a glide or even a swim then the legs will be forced downwards in what can be described as a 'Seesaw' movement. If the head twists from side to side, the body will also twist from side to side. Therefore it is easier to emphasise the stillness of the head!

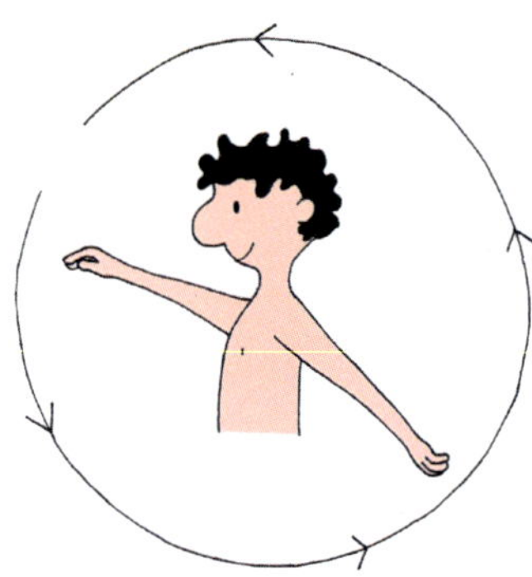

If the pupil is having difficulty co-ordinating the circles the practise can be made easier if you stand face-to-face and also do the big slow circles and role model the actions and encourage copying! Young children especially can benefit from this 'mirroring' style practise as they can see exactly what it should look like.

### STEP 2:- The feel of the water.

Once the circles can be performed in a controlled and correct manner, out of the pool, the learner is ready to progress into the pool. However we are not going to swim just yet! Firstly stand the pupil up in water no deeper than their chest level. Attempt the circle practise once again exactly as we learned at home. Encourage the pupil to stand up straight, with both feet together, and arms out stretched in front of their face looking down the 'Centre Line' towards the point where their hands meet. Reinforce the big slow circular movements that are needed and try to ensure that the child's hand enters the water very slowly with little or no splash. If a splash is present this is a clear sign that the learner is rushing.

Now the pupil will begin to experience what is called the 'Feel of the Water'. This is where the hand pulls through the water and is what will in the next stage lead to the propulsion needed for a successful swim. Emphasise the fact that one half of the circle should be done under water and the other half should be done above the water. If the circles are big and slow the hands on entry to the water should make little or no splash.

What we wish to avoid is a slapping sound of the hand as it enters into the water. This will prove counterproductive and will waste energy at both this stage and later stages. The hand should enter the water on the 'Centre Line' in a smooth and controlled manner. To assist the pupil, it would be a good idea for you to stand face to face with them once again and check that they are indeed landing on the 'Centre Line'. If needs be continue the 'mirror style' copying practise where you take the lead.

## STEP 3:- At last, the swim! Big circles, smooth circles!

By this stage our learner should be confident in the water and able to perform a controlled submersion of the face, a star float and a glide with a kick. They should also have a sound understanding of how to perform a controlled circular arm movement.

Find a suitable area of the pool, once again shallow water is what we need, no deeper than chest level on the child. The quieter the area the better, facing the roman steps or poolside would be ideal but no more than the equivalent of two of the pupil's body lengths away. Encourage our learner to take up a gliding position in the shallow water, to take a huge breath, to put their face in the water. To push and glide, then to kick with their legs and finally, without moving their head, to use their circles and their centre line. If all other stages have been followed successfully the swim should prove relatively easy and should look quite calm!

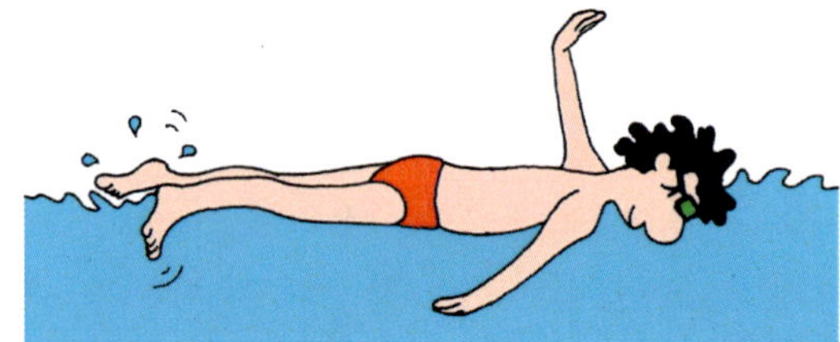

As far as the distance is concerned, as confidence grows by all means allow the pupil to increase the distance little by little. Also remind them that they can stand up and end the practise as soon as they wish. To do this they simply lift their head out of the water and pull both knee's up towards their chest before finally stamping their feet to the bottom of the pool.

Remember always ensure that they feel in control of the situation. What we must bear in mind is the fact that a swimmer can only swim so far without taking on board a fresh supply of oxygen. Therefore we should not increase the distance too much as panic will set in. As a guide, a swim without a breath need not be more than six circles in length and the swimmer should not end the swim by gasping for breath. If this occurs the swim was a little too far. Focus on quality not on quantity and the smoothness of the arm action and achieving the correct flat body position.

Key Phrases:- Big Breath, Big Circles, Slow Circles, Touch the Centre Line and Keep the Head Still.

## FREQUENTLY ASKED QUESTIONS

### 1.) Why touch the 'Centre Line?

As well as the reasons mentioned above the stroke should be symmetrical. What one side of the body does the other should do in equal measure. If one arm pulls further than the other, the stroke will suffer. If a swimmer begins each and every circle on the 'Centre Line', upper body symmetry will be achieved and the swim will be all the better for it!

### 2.) When my Child swims her hands make a big splash. How can I stop this happening?

It sounds quite simple. Firstly I would advise you to encourage a slow swim. A big splash usually means that the hand is entering the water at speed. Secondly try to get your daughter's hands to enter the water fingertips first.

### 3.) I've seen top swimmers on the television and they don't seem to use the 'Circles' that you have taught us. Why is this?

You are correct! Good Front Crawl swimmers do not keep their arms straight and make circles. However we are dealing with beginners and circles are far easier to learn. Once our learner becomes competent the stroke can easily be adapted if you wish!

### 4.) Why is the stroke called 'Front Crawl'?

I believe it is because the under water movements of the hands resemble a crawling action as you would see with a baby crawling on the floor! When performing the stroke the swimmer is also on their swimming on their front, hence the term 'Front Crawl'. If I am wrong, please let me know!

### 5.) My son's circles start off really smooth but soon turn very splashy. Why is this and how can I stop it?

This is a commonly seen indicator that a child is trying to swim too far! What happens is that he or she gradually runs out of breath as the swim progresses and as they feel this happen, they try to rush the swim to finish sooner. I would stop the swim once you see the first signs of this increase in speed. Remember we are only looking for between four and six huge slow circles. You could also ensure that he is getting a huge breath at the start of the swim.

# Chapter Four

## Learning to breathe.

At this stage our pupil should be able to glide, kick and perform circles in a controlled and confident manner for a distance of between four and six circles whilst demonstrating a good streamlined body position. Now begins the tricky part! The most important aspect of learning to swim, without a shadow of doubt, is to be able to breathe when needed and without stopping the stroke to do so.

Put simply breathing determines the distance that a swimmer can swim. I compare breathing and swimming to petrol and cars! The concept is the same and most children when asked will say that if a car does not have much petrol it will not travel very far before coming to a stop! Timing and technique are also crucial aspects of the hardest lesson we will have to learn in this program! As with everything we have learned so far we are going to keep things as simple as we can. We will also revisit and build upon some of the skills learned in lesson one.

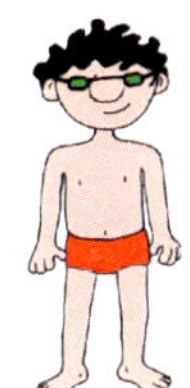

### STEP 1:- Back to bubbles and learning to twist!

During Lesson One we looked at how to perform a controlled submersion of the face. We focussed on the 'big breath' and we then moved on to blowing bubbles. These two aspects now come back to our attention and will form an important part of our breathing technique.

To start introduce the basics out of the water, at home or maybe sat on the poolside. We want our learner to understand the concept of the twist. To do this sit them up right in a comfortable position facing forwards. Ideally sit them in front of something that may be of interest, for example, a window, a swimming pool rescue buoy or maybe even their bag. If you make sure that you are in front of them tell them to look at you then to look at the chosen object behind them. Then tell them to look at you and so on. Their twisting action should come naturally and should be performed in a controlled manner and slowly to avoid injury. Also you must ensure that the learner is only expected to twist far enough behind them to perform the practise but not to cause any discomfort or pain whatsoever.

Now into the water! Once again we are looking for shallow water and a quiet area of the pool if possible. Either the poolside or roman style steps would be ideal. The pupil should either kneel down or crouch down with their knees bent and both hands on the poolside or the top roman step. The arms should be as straight as possible and on the surface of the water with the hands shoulder width apart. As soon as this position has been achieved we are ready to begin.

There are four areas that we are going to focus on to introduce breathing and as always we will keep it simple. Begin by positioning yourself on the favoured side of the pupil i.e. their left or right hand side. Remind them of the twisting practise already performed. We then need the pupil to:-

1.) Get a huge big breath and to submerge the face calmly into the water between the arms and to blow as many bubbles as they can.

2.) As soon as they reach the point where they have blown most of their bubbles, they should be encouraged to twist their head to their favourite side and look at you so make sure that you are on the correct side! If this twist is done correctly the ear on the non-favoured side should be in the water. The mouth should just come clear enough from the water to ensure that none is swallowed.

3.) It is now that the pupil should take the biggest inward breath that they can.

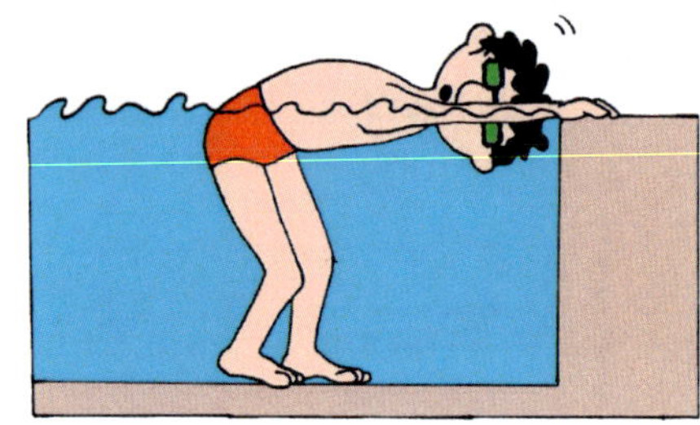

4.) Finally our learner should twist their face back into the water and start all over again.

Focus on big bubbles, a big breath and a controlled twist of the head both in and out of the water. Most importantly the pupil should never lift their head and look forwards.

If there is even the slightest element of lift when performing the twist the lower corner of the mouth will be submerged and the swimmer will swallow water. There is also more chance of water being forced up the nose upon re-entry which is less than pleasant. If this lift occurred when actually swimming, as we mentioned earlier in the series, like a seesaw, if the head goes up, the legs will be forced downwards and the streamlined position will be ruined. Therefore it is far better to really concentrate on a well executed technical twist of the head and shoulders from the beginning. This stage could also be practised in the bath but always with supervision.

Key Phrases:- Big breath, big bubbles, a controlled twist of the head, ear in the water, twist the shoulders to and don't lift the head.

## STEP 2:- Bubbles, twisting and kicking!

Once STEP 1 has been practised several times, and can be performed without error, we are ready for a slight progression. This progression is in physical difficulty rather than technical difficulty. This practise should be done in the same part of the pool as the kneeling or crouching practice. However this time we are aiming to carry on the good work from STEP 1 but, instead of kneeling or crouching, we are going to encourage the pupil to attempt to perform a good leg kick at the same time.

The idea of the progression is to improve performance and this practice is probably the hardest of all the ones that we have looked at so far. Once mastered it will ensure the pupil's breathing is strong and without fault. Therefore, simply repeat all of the technical aspects learned in STEP 1 but ensure a good 'drum roll' style leg kick. Remember, straight legs, toes pointed in tip toe position and a small alternating kick. If the kick is too big, or too slow, the body position will not be correct as the legs will be sinking.

As with the glide the body position should be flat and outstretched on top of the water, without allowing the feet to touch the floor. The idea now is to build stamina and strength in the practice whilst continuing to develop the actual breathing. See how many breaths the pupil can do on their first attempt and then simply try to do more and more breaths per attempt but, as always, without pupil our learner under any pressure.

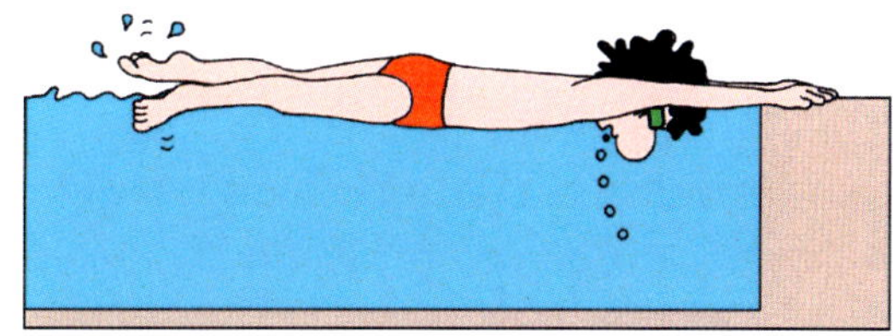

Key Phrases:- 'Good leg kick', 'big bubbles', 'twist the head and shoulders', 'big breath in'.

### STEP 3:- Counting to Four!!

Once STEP 2 has been mastered we are going to make one important adjustment, a final tweak if you will! This adjustment is to prepare our learner for the next and final lesson. Begin by revisiting the kneeling/crouching version of the breathing practise. This time when the pupil submerges their face tell them that they have until you have counted to four to blow their bubbles, no less and no more. In fact, it is a good idea if you count loudly up to four from your position on their favoured side. You could also put your hand underwater and within their line of sight and count up to four with your fingers as you say the words just to reinforce the number four.

Why four you may be thinking? Put simply that is the breathing pattern that I would like to introduce when we come to put the swimming and breathing together. Four big circles with bubbles and the breathing followed by another four circles and so on and so on. Some Swimming Instructors teach their learners to breath after two circles and some six.

I always teach a beginner to breathe on a breathing pattern of four circles ( i.e. a breath after every fourth circle) because breathing after two circles would be too often and will disrupt the beginner by not letting them settle into their swim. Also a beginner will only be swimming short distances and will not need to breathe so often. A top class swimmer may well have to breathe on every two arm pulls as they are burning up oxygen at an alarming rate. We do not have this problem!

Ok, well why not breathe after every six circles you may ask? Breathing after every six circles is in my opinion, too far to go without oxygen, especially for a child. We never want panic to set in. Panic is something we always want to avoid. Therefore four circles will allow our swimmer to settle into their stroke and breathe without ever panicking. Panic in this case is caused by what we call an ‘oxygen debt’, which is the stage at which the brain wonders why the oxygen supply has been cut off and sends signals of alarm and distress to the body. It basically tells it to stop and stand up and gasp in oxygen. This ‘panic state’ is easily avoided if we encourage our learner to swim slow, take regular big breathes and to focus on quality small swims rather than focussing on distance for the sake of a badge! Badges and distance will come as our learner improves their skills and their stamina.

## STEP 4:- The use of buoyancy aides in the development of the breathing.

There are many different types of buoyancy aids available on the market today and indeed for loan at your local pool. I would recommend the use of a buoyancy aid to ensure the continuing development of the breathing and to improve stamina and strength in the legs. My personal preference would be to use one of the long tubular foam floats known as woggles. In my experience they give far better balance and stability than the more traditional rectangular foam floats, which are usually used to strengthen and improve the kick for more advanced swimmers only.

We began to breathe by holding the poolside or the roman steps and kneeling or crouching on the pool bottom. We then progressed to kicking and breathing in a stationary position on the poolside and now we come to the last stage before we combine swimming and breathing. This practise involves the same technique as the breathing practise where we held the poolside or roman steps and performed the kick. The only difference is that we are going to be holding the float and therefore moving across the water.

If the pupil is using the tubular float their hands should be in the middle of the float and shoulder width apart. If they are using the rectangular float their hands should be holding on to the bottom corners rather than reaching over to the furthest corners and resting their forearms on the float itself.

As I have said throughout we only need shallow water to perform our practises. However, we do now need to increase our distances, without encroaching into deeper water. Several widths in shallow water is far safer than two lengths that go into deeper water. That said, we can begin.

Encourage our pupil to take up their ‘gliding feet’ position. The float should be held outstretched in front of the face with their arms straight and their chin touching the water. Give the instructions ‘big breath, face in and push and glide’. As soon as the feet come up off the floor the kick must begin. Initially stand on the pupil’s favoured side and walk alongside them, holding the float with one hand and gently pull the float just to take some pressure off the pupils leg kick. When in this position you are also ideally positioned to count loudly and say 'one, two, three, four, breathe'. Thereby reminding and reinforcing the breathing pattern. Everything else remains the same as it was when we practised breathing holding onto the poolside. Ensure that our learners ear is in the water when they twist and that they swallow no water.

Key Phrases:- 'Good leg kick', 'straight arms', 'count to four when blowing the bubbles' and a good twist.

Frequently Asked Questions.

1.) Why do you always emphasise shallow water?

Whether you are performing a glide, a breathing practise on the float or indeed swimming, your body should only use the top few inches of the water. Therefore why seek out deep water! It's not needed. Also for beginners it may cause nervousness that may well distract them from the practise at hand.

2.) Why should I assist the pupil by pulling the float?

The physical difficulty involved in the breathing practise on the float is due to the fact that the legs are providing all of the propulsion. You may remember during lesson two, I said that in the front crawl the majority of the propulsion comes from the arms. Therefore these leg muscles are working extremely hard and will tire soon, at least for beginners. By giving assistance in these early stages, you will save the pupil wasting energy and help improve the practise by keeping momentum up.

3.) Why is a breathing pattern important?

A breathing pattern is vital for several reasons. When we swim with our face in the water we cannot breathe, therefore our oxygen supply is limited. This means that we must take regular opportunities to breathe in order to maintain an oxygen supply. If we swim too far without breathing we run the risk of incurring an 'oxygen debt' which will lead to panic. Swimming with a regular breathing pattern ensures that regular breathing becomes a habit and this is a good thing. Distance swimming is all about fooling the brain that nothing has changed and that oxygen is in plentiful supply.

### 4.) Why do you recommend breathing after every four circles?

Taking a regular breath is vital to ensure that the swimmer is comfortable during the swim and never enters a 'panic state'. However a swimmer can breathe too often. For example, if a swimmer breathes after every two circles, when swimming only a short distance, the oxygen supplies in the body will not have been burned up and the stroke may be disrupted unnecessarily. A top class distance swimmer may need to breathe after every two circles as they will indeed be burning up vast amounts of oxygen. However, breathing after every six circles may be too much for our pupil who may end up panicking, something which we also want to avoid. Therefore breathing after ever four circles has always seemed ideal to me as it is right in the middle! So treat four as our magic number and make sure that four is counted to before our pupil turns to get their breath.

# Chapter Five

## Putting the swimming and the breathing together!

Firstly may I say congratulations on getting to this stage. I can appreciate how much effort and time it has taken but remember, if you continue to practise and reinforce what has been learned so far it will never be forgotten. Now all that we have learned so far must be pulled together. From the big breath and the glide to the circles and the breathing as well as everything in between! As with everything else we have gone through so far let's keep it simple and let's enjoy it!

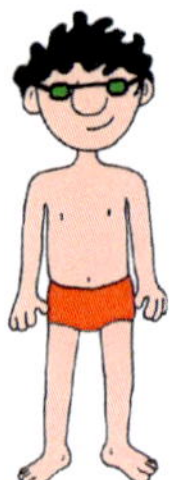

### STEP 1:- A recap and warm up!

A quick recap and warm up would be a good starting point for all of the lessons from now on. Begin with a few glides with a leg kick, moving on to some small swims and finish with some assisted breathing exercises on the float (assisted in that you gently pull the float not to make the pupil overwork during the warm up).

Key Phrases:- Big breath, face in, push and glide, kick and big slow circles.

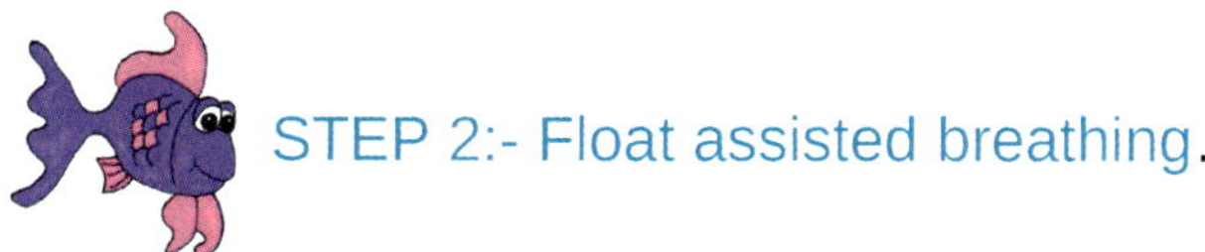

## STEP 2:- Float assisted breathing.

Whether you are using the tubular float, or the rectangular float, encourage our learner to hold it with their non-favoured hand. If using the tubular float hold it in the centre. If using the rectangular float hold it in the centre between the two corners nearest the pupil. Our pupil must now get their gliding feet ready and hold the float out straight, in front of their face, with their holding hand on their 'Centre Line' (the invisible line that goes out from the nose and splits the body into two). Their favoured arm is going to be used to perform circles, but for the glide it can be kept next to the hand that is holding the float in order to maintain a streamlined position. Once it is needed it can simply slide off the float and begin to make the circles.

Give the usual instructions, 'big breath, face in, push, glide and kick' and tell the pupil that after the short glide, they need to perform four big slow circles but ONLY with their favoured arm. This will feel strange but is easy to get used to. As each circle comes back into the water it must brush against the other hand, and thereby touch the 'Centre Line'. As with the breathing practise on the float, that we learned in the previous lesson, you can stand on the favoured side of the pupil and gently pull the float if needed, in order to keep up momentum.

You can also count the circles, verbally or by placing your hand under water in the pupil's line of sight and count the pattern on your fingers, just to remind the pupil and reinforce the rhythm. Ideally, combine both methods! By the time that the pupil gets to circle number three they should have almost blown out all of their bubbles. When circle number four is just finishing the underwater part of the stroke, and rising up to the surface (what we swim teachers call the upsweep!), they must perform their well practised twist of the head and shoulder. Ensuring that their face comes out of the water at exactly the same time as the circle hand does. Remember the ear on their non-favoured side must sit in the water as a direct result of the twist. For example if they are right handed as their right hand comes out of the water, on circle four, their left ear will be in the water. Remind the pupil that they must not lift their head and look forwards at any stage.

Part 1- Our learner blows their controlled bubbles as they perform the slow big circles with their favoured arm.

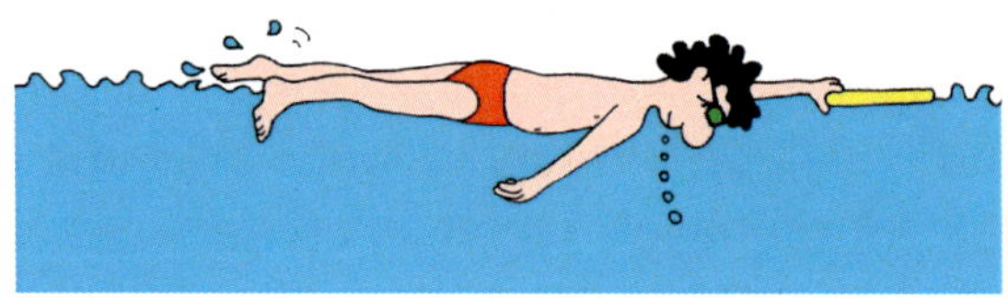

Part 2- Our learner should twist their upper body towards their 'circle' arm as circle four comes out of the water.

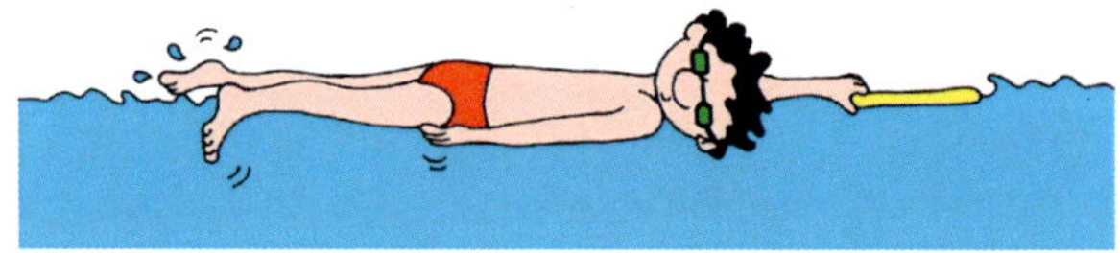

Part 3- Our learner then has to start breathing as soon as their face and circle arm come out of the water.

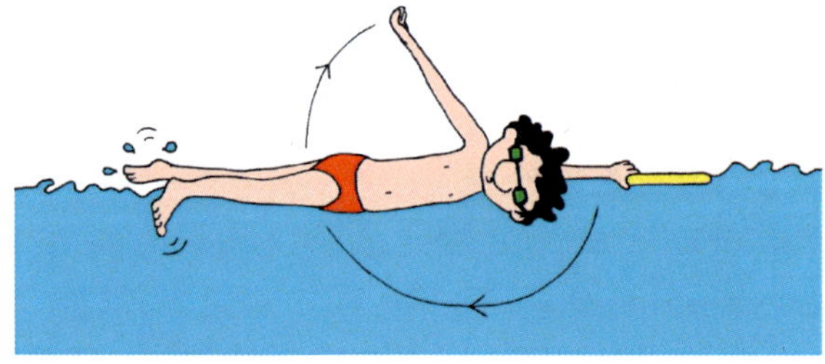

Part 4- Remember they must look to their favoured side when breathing and never ever forwards.

Part 5- Our learner has from the time the hand comes out of the water until it re-enters the water to get their breath. Therefore the face and hand should enter the water at exactly the same time.

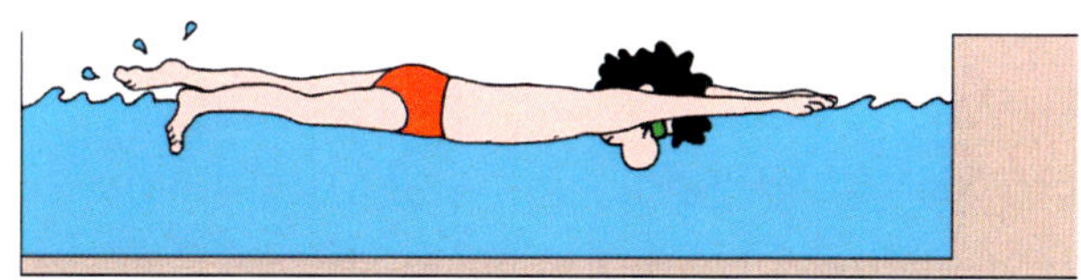

This is why we have always emphasised big slow circles. Obviously the more time a swimmer has to breathe the better, although one should never pause or stop the circle to gain more breathing time. If this does happen and the hand stops above the body, the centre of buoyancy will alter, and the pupil will begin to sink due to the weight of the arm when out of the water.

I always tell my pupils that a good swimmer fits their breathing into their circles. A common fault is for the pupil to swim with a suitable rhythm but to spoil it by slowing or stopping the breathing arm as it passes over the head on circle four. Granted from the time the hand leaves the water until the time it re-enters may only be a split second, but if the bubbles have been blown and the head is in the correct place, this split second gives more than enough opportunity to gain the 'big breath' needed.

Once one breath has been mastered with float support, attempt to build on this by increasing the distance. Four circles breathe, four circles breathe and so on. As always widths in shallow water are safer than lengths that go through deep water.

## STEP 3:- Swimming and breathing without assistance.

Everything we have learned so far has been building up to this moment. By now our pupil can swim and our pupil can breathe. However they cannot yet swim and breathe! Breathing is the most important part of swimming as it determines the distance that a swimmer can swim and the way in which they will swim. A swimmer who has a good grasp of breathing will almost always have a better stroke than a swimmer who does not, as they will be less likely to panic. A swimmer who panics because they struggle to breathe will usually have a rushed, slap dash stroke which is counter productive and will never allow the pupil to enjoy their swimming. Our pupil will however have learned the correct way and should never fall into this category!

Our learner begins their swim in the usual way, with a big breath, a glide, a kick and the big slow circles. Make sure that their circles begin with their non-favoured hand, the left hand if they are right handed and vice versa. Stand on their favoured side and count each circle loudly, whilst walking along side them. Just as we did on the float practise, encourage the pupil to blow slow and controlled bubbles until circle number four is just about to leave the water.

They then perform the 'twist' and ensure that the face comes out of the water at exactly the same time as the hand leaves the water, on the fourth circle, as they did on the float. They then have the time it takes for the fourth circle to pass over the head and re-enter the water to get their breath. As with the float practise, ensure that the circles are not slowed down or the rhythm altered at all. Remember it is the swimmer who must fit the breathing into the circles.

When standing on the swimmers favoured side, as they breathe, you should be able to see their face as they take the breath and they should be able to see you. You should also be able to hear the breath as it is taken in. If the breath is big enough, it will make a noise like a gasp and this is good!

This 'gasp' should finish just before the face re-enters the water, which when timed to perfection will happen just as the hand re-enters the water. The swimmer then continues with another four circles and so on. Realistically this final step will take some practise and always begin your training sessions with a recap in the form of a warm-up. Four circles breathe, four circles breathe then becomes further and further until everything clicks into place and finally comes the stamina work. This is just an increase in the distances you expect your pupil to complete, a sort of fitness training!

Make a game of it. After every session remember how many breaths were taken without a break and then try to beat that record at the next session, but always in shallow water. Remember always keep it safe and always keep it fun. We do not need deep water to improve a swimmer's stoke or stamina. For example, if your local pool is 10 metres wide and 25 metres long, it is better to attempt to swim ten widths in the shallow end than two lengths which go through deep water.

I hope that both you and our pupil have enjoyed the lessons and feel that they have been of benefit. Whether it has taken three weeks, or twelve months, what you have achieved together should give you both a sense of pride. Learning to swim is not easy but it doesn't have to be too difficult either. Likewise teaching someone to swim is not easy but it can be done if the key stages are broken down, and kept simple, as we have both proved. Well done and keep swimming!!

Key phrases:- Finish the bubbles by circle number four, the face comes out of the water as the fourth circle comes out, the face re-enters the water as the 'breathing circle' re-enters.

## FREQUENTLY ASKED QUESTIONS.

1.) What happens if the float is not held in the centre?

If the grip on the float is off centre the float will tip over. This is not the end of the world but it will affect the streamlined position. Remember let's do everything we can to make things easy and streamlined means easier!

2.) What if water is swallowed when breathing?

Unfortunately this does happen and goes hand in hand with learning to breathe. Every effort should be made to ensure that water is not swallowed. Follow all of steps carefully. However, if water is swallowed stand the pupil up immediately and encourage them to cough. Make every effort to keep them calm. If they see you panic chances are they will panic all the more. If needs be call for the assistance of the lifeguard. It is very rare that swallowed water is not cured by coughing. Coughing is the body's unique method of removing the water that has been swallowed unintentionally. However if our learner is sick, or continues coughing for a longer period than you feel normal, liaise with the Life Guard team and seek medical assistance.

### 3.) Why emphasise 'big bubbles'?

When we blow out and make 'big bubbles' in the water and then turn to breathe, we trigger off a natural bodily reaction called a 'gag reflex'. This 'gag reflex' encourages the body to get the biggest breath it can as soon as it can. If the bubbles are half hearted, chances are, the inward breath will be half hearted also and the swim will soon turn into a panic swim.

### 4.) What if the pupil forgets to blow bubbles altogether?

When the pupil turns to breathe their lungs will still be full of air and, although the oxygen will have been sent around the body, there will be little room to accommodate an inward breath. Breathing begins with bubbles!

# Appendix

Below are a set of printable awards designed to encourage your child in the early stages of learning to swim.

These awards are free, simply visit **www.theswimmingteacher.com** to download and print.

Award 1

Award 2

Award 3

Made in the USA
Las Vegas, NV
13 June 2022